A GOLDEN **EXPLORING EARTH** BOOK

Reptiles and Amphibians

**A close look at two fascinating groups of animals.
Amphibians: frogs, toads, and salamanders.
Reptiles: turtles, lizards, snakes, alligators, and crocodiles—
all shown in color.**

**By Matt Warner
Cover by Rod Ruth**

gb® . **GOLDEN PRESS**

Western Publishing Company, Inc.   Racine, Wisconsin

Copyright © 1974 by Western Publishing Company, Inc.
Illustrations on pages 5, 16, 17 from WATCH THEM GROW UP
© 1959 by Row, Peterson and Company; pages 5, 10, 11 from TOADS AND FROGS
copyright 1942 by Row, Peterson and Company; pages 23,25,26,31, 34
from REPTILES copyright 1942 by Row, Peterson and Company; title page
from HOW ANIMALS GET FOOD © 1959 by Row, Peterson and Company.

Reptiles and Amphibians

Reptiles and amphibians are probably the most misunderstood animals in the world. Sometimes the facts about these interesting animals are difficult to separate from the many myths and legends. Some stories show them as evil, dangerous beasts or as having supernatural powers. Crocodiles and alligators are giants, it's true, and they are commonly ill-tempered—no more approachable than an angry bull. It is also true that some snakes, frogs, and toads are poisonous. However, most of the many kinds of reptiles and amphibians are harmless. A number of them are even directly helpful to human life, and all of them fit importantly into nature's overall plan, as does every living thing.

Of the five principal groups of animals with backbones—mammals, birds, reptiles, amphibians, and fishes—reptiles occupy the middle position. Amphibians are a step lower in the scale of life. They come between reptiles and fishes. Among animals with backbones, they are the lowest form, or group, that can live on land, for, as adults, most kinds of amphibians have lungs and can breathe air. They spend at least a part of their lives in water, however, and at this stage, like fishes, they have gills.

Amphibians are most abundant, both in numbers and kinds, in warm, moist climates. They are cold-blooded animals. Their body temperature varies with the temperature of their surroundings. It is not kept at some constant high level by internal regulation, as it is in birds and mammals. Those few kinds of amphibians that live in cold, temperate regions hibernate during the winter months.

Because they have moist skins, amphibians must live either in water or in very moist areas to keep from drying out. Those that live where there are many dry months during the year dig deep burrows to get to moisture and may also become dormant during the dry period. Even toads, the most land-dwelling of the amphibians, return to water to lay their eggs, and their young develop in water, breathing with gills before they become air breathers.

Reptiles are better equipped for life on land. They have a dry outer covering of either scales or plates. This prevents loss of their body fluids, permitting them to live far from water—even in hot, dry climates. Their eggs have a tough shell and do not have to be in water. Some kinds of reptiles hold their eggs inside their body until they hatch, then "give birth" to their young. Like the adults, the young reptiles breathe with lungs, which are more efficient in removing carbon dioxide and in taking in oxygen than either the gills or the primitive lungs of the amphibians.

But reptiles are still cold-blooded animals. They are common in regions from warm to tropical. Those that live in temperate regions survive the cold winters by hibernating.

In the past, during the years of the Coal Age swamps, about 350 million years ago, amphibians were the dominant animals on earth. They were the first animals to invade the land, but in distribution, they were limited to moist regions. When reptiles appeared, they soon became the dominant animals, because they could inhabit a greater range of land areas—the dry as well as the moist.

Extinct Reptiles and Amphibian

Dinosaurs

Amphibian

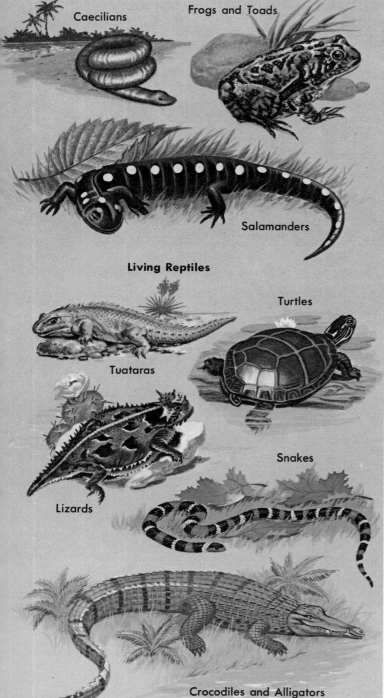

Living Amphibians

Caecilians

Frogs and Toads

Salamanders

Living Reptiles

Tuataras

Turtles

Lizards

Snakes

Crocodiles and Alligators

The most famous of the prehistoric reptiles were the dinosaurs. Most of the many kinds were not much larger than chickens, but some were giants—the largest animals that have ever lived on land. When great changes took place in the earth's climate, these very specialized reptiles were not able to adjust to the new conditions, and they were not matches for the more intelligent birds and mammals. Most of the ancient reptiles disappeared.

Of the many kinds and great variety of amphibians that existed in the past, there are only three groups today: (1) the caecilians, which are small, legless, wormlike animals of the tropics; (2) frogs and toads, which have four legs and no tail; and (3) salamanders and newts, which are slim, long-tailed, and typically four-legged. Similarly, the reptiles are represented today by far fewer and less varied types than in the geologic past. The five surviving groups are: (1) the odd tuataras, primitive creatures found only on islands off the northern coast of New Zealand; (2) turtles, easily identified by their shells; (3) lizards, which typically have four legs and a distinct tail; (4) snakes, which are legless; and (5) the giant crocodiles and alligators.

Bullfrog

Frogs—Amphibians Without Tails

Everyone knows what frogs and toads look like. They are squat, tailless creatures that can jump long distances with their powerful hind legs. But how does a frog differ from a toad?

The typical frogs live in or near water, and they have moist skins. The typical toads spend their adult lives on land, often far from water, and they have dry, rough, usually warty skins.

Both frogs and toads lay their eggs in water. The young, called tadpoles, live in the water, with gills for breathing. A tadpole, at first, has no legs, but it does have a tail. As the tadpole changes gradually into its adult form, the tail disappears, and legs develop, first the front and then the back. At the same time, the gills, too, disappear, and the animal acquires lungs for breathing air. These are some of the many changes that take place as the tadpole becomes an adult.

The bullfrog, the largest and one of the most familiar of all North American frogs, lives in ponds, marshes, and swampy lowlands. In spring, the males give off low, deep-throated, booming calls as loud as a pig's grunts. This is the mating call. As soon as the females lay their eggs in the water, the males fertilize them. In a week, or longer if the water is cool, the eggs hatch, and a swarm of tiny black tadpoles emerges.

Bullfrog tadpoles become very large—some as long as six inches. In northern regions, it may require as much as three

Leopard Frog

5

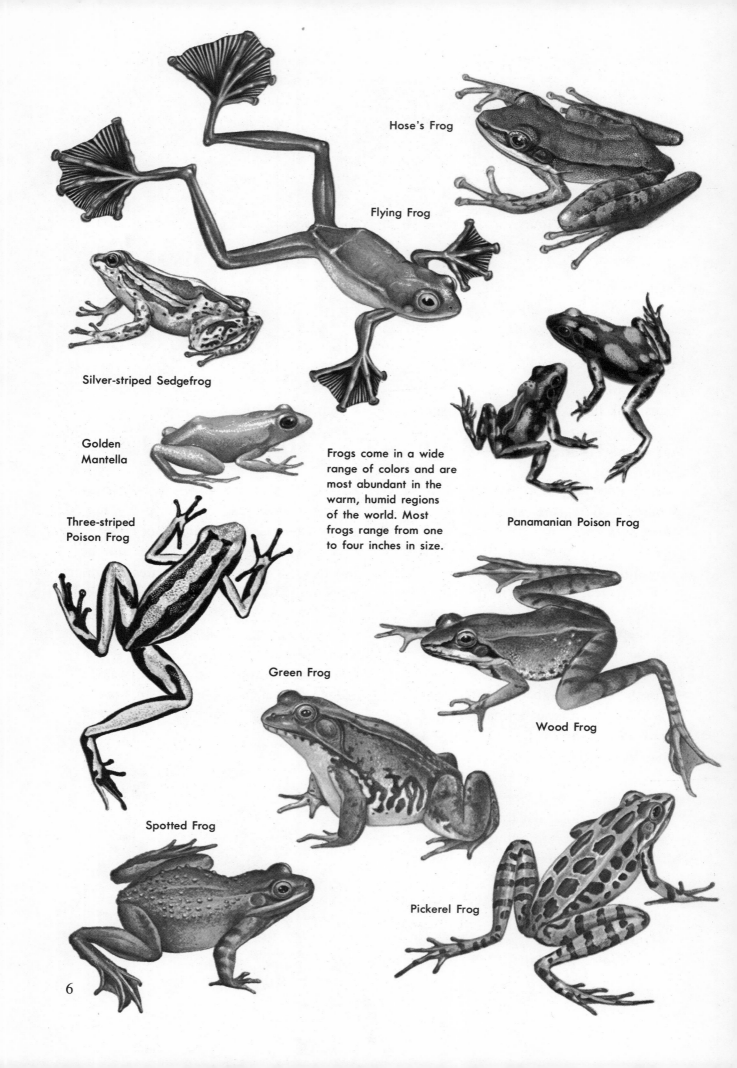

Hose's Frog

Flying Frog

Silver-striped Sedgefrog

Golden Mantella

Three-striped Poison Frog

Frogs come in a wide range of colors and are most abundant in the warm, humid regions of the world. Most frogs range from one to four inches in size.

Panamanian Poison Frog

Green Frog

Wood Frog

Spotted Frog

Pickerel Frog

6

years for them to complete their growth and change into the adult form. A full-grown bullfrog may be more than a foot long when its big hind legs are fully stretched.

The more common, handsome leopard frog, less than four inches long, has round, leopardlike spots on its metallic green body. Two yellowish or bronze patches extend from behind each eye to the end of its body. The leopard frog is a more melodious singer than the bullfrog. Both produce their calls from pouches that swell up just behind and below the ears. When not in use, these bags look like wrinkled folds of skin.

The very similar pickerel frog, found only in eastern North America, has square or rectangular spots rather than round ones. Its legs are tinged with red or orange; the leopard frog's are greenish.

Not all frogs are so "typical" in appearance. The three-inch spotted frog that lives in northwestern North America has a rough, warty skin, much like a toad's, but it is moist. The wood frog, of northeastern United States and Canada, is a warm brown color, like an autumn leaf. Its cheeks are black, and it has a strong yellow line along the upper jaw. This is perfect camouflage, for the wood frog prefers moist woods to meadows and ponds. The most land-loving of all the frogs in North America, it has the strange habit of turning in midair when it leaps, so that it lands facing the direction from which it took off.

Some of the many kinds of frogs of the tropics and subtropics are unusually colorful. The golden mantella, for example, is bright orange, which is quite a contrast to the green usually thought of as a frog's color. The tree-dwelling flying frog of southeastern Asia and nearby islands has broad webs between its exceptionally long toes. When it leaps from a tree, the flying frog spreads its toes so that the webs act as sails or parachutes, helping it to glide for long distances or to make a soft, safe landing on the ground.

Darwin's Frog

Australian Burrower Frog

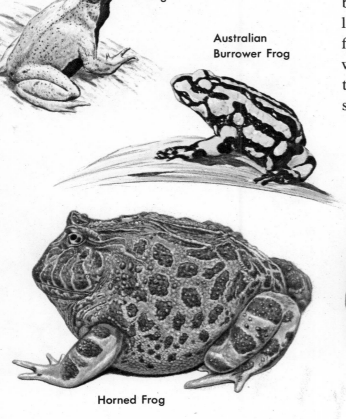

Horned Frog

Goliath Frog

Robber Frog

Ornate Chorus Frog Strecker's Chorus Frog

Cricket Frog Swamp Chorus Frog

Flying frogs lay their eggs on leaves over pools of water. When the eggs hatch, the squirming tadpoles wriggle off the leaves and fall into the water below. With the broad suction cups on their toes, the adults can hold on to vertical surfaces for climbing. This is also true of the silver-striped sedgefrog, hose's frog, and other tree frogs, of which there are many kinds in the tropics and subtropics.

The three-striped poison frog lives in the South American jungles. The Panamanian poison frog lives in the jungles of Central America. Both produce a strong poison in the glands in their skin.

Like many other tree frogs, the young of these frogs begin their lives in the small pools of water that collect in the hollows of trees, where the females lay their eggs. When an adult frog enters a pool containing tadpoles, some of the young grab hold with their mouths and hang on for a free ride to a new pool. In this unusual way, the tadpoles get to a new supply of food and are also spread from place to place.

The Australian burrower frog spends the many dry months of the year in a deep underground burrow. It stores a large amount of water in its baggy body before going into its burrow. The closely related South American horned frog is a nine-inch warty creature that has teeth large enough to draw blood. It snaps at anything that comes close and can stuff astonishingly large animals into its cavernous mouth.

The sharp-snouted Darwin's frog, also of South America, is unusual in that the males carry the eggs in the oversized vocal pouches that stretch the full length of their body. The eggs hatch and develop inside these pouches. When they emerge, they are fully developed little frogs.

The giant of the clan is the African goliath frog, with a body as much as ten inches long. The smallest, less than an

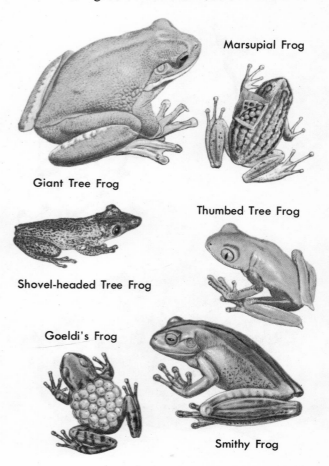

Marsupial Frog

Giant Tree Frog

Thumbed Tree Frog

Shovel-headed Tree Frog

Goeldi's Frog

Smithy Frog

Squirrel Tree Frog	Pacific Tree Frog	Common Tree Frog	Green Tree Frog

Spring Peeper	Whistling Tree Frog	Canyon Tree Frog	Pine Tree Frog

inch long, are the little robber frogs of the American tropics and subtropics, one kind ranging into southern United States.

Many of the tree frogs, widely distributed throughout the world, are less than two inches long. The largest is a giant Australian tree frog that is more than five inches long. It may be matched in size, however, by the Cuban tree frog, ranging from extreme southern United States into the tropics.

Most of the frogs in this group, which includes the cricket frogs and the chorus frogs, have surprisingly loud voices for such small animals. They can turn a spring or summer night into a deafening clamor of piercing, trilling calls. The "smithy" frog gets its name from the metallic ring of its call, which is like the sound of a hammer striking an anvil.

Cricket and chorus frogs lack toe pads. They spend most of their time on the ground. The canyon tree frog, one of the most aquatic of all frogs, emerges from the water only occasionally to climb the rocky canyon walls.

Marsupial frogs are the most unusual of the tree frogs. The females carry their eggs in pouches on their back. In some, the young come out of these pouches while they are still in the tadpole stage. In others, the tadpole has already become a small frog by the time it emerges. The female Goeldi's frog lacks a pouch. She holds her eggs between folds of skin on her back. In another strange group of tree frogs, the head is covered with a hard, bonelike helmet of skin. The shovel-headed tree frog of Mexico and Central America belongs to this group.

American Toad

Toads—More Tailless Amphibians

Toads, like frogs, are widely distributed over the world. They live wherever the summers are warm and wherever there is enough water nearby in which their young can grow. The female typical toad lays her eggs in a double string. Each egg is encased in a jellylike substance so that the strings look like beads. In contrast, the typical frogs lay eggs in a clump or a mass.

The American toad is found throughout eastern North America. Females may produce as many as 10,000 eggs every spring. In warm water, these eggs may hatch in as short a time as three days. If the water is cool, it may require two weeks or longer. The tadpoles are usually

Spadefoot Toad

Midwife Toad

Fowler's Toad

10

large enough to grow into tiny toads within two or three months.

A toad's tongue is attached at the front of its mouth. When a toad sees something moving nearby, it opens its mouth and flips out its tongue. The movement is so quick that you will miss it if you blink your eyes. The tongue curls around the object and draws it back into the toad's mouth, where it is swallowed whole.

Fowler's toad is slightly smaller than the American toad. It is greener and has a distinct line down its back. It is the western version of the American toad.

The largest of the toads is the marine toad of the American tropics and subtropics. Its body may be as much as nine inches long, but because it is so wide and bulky, it appears to be even larger. The marine toad has been taken into many farming regions to live and help control insects. It has a tremendous appetite and will gobble anything that moves in its path. But there is one danger: the poison from this big toad's skin glands is powerful. It has been known to kill dogs and other animals that have tried to eat it.

The smallest of the typical toads of North America is the little oak toad, generally only about an inch long. Like other toads, the male expands its throat pouch like a big bubble when it "sings" at mating time in spring.

The three-inch spadefoot toad of southern and western North America has spadelike projections on its hind legs. These are worked like shovels in soft dirt. If you put a spadefoot toad on the sand in front of you, it seems to sink out of sight as it works its feet and buries itself. Most of the burrows in which these toads live are only about six inches long, but some of the burrows are as much as three feet deep. The toads come out only at night.

The midwife toad, a two-inch toad that lives in southwestern Europe, takes care

Oak Toad

Marine Toad

Fire-bellied Toad

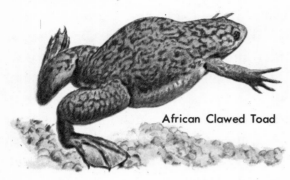

African Clawed Toad

Surinam Toad

Zetek's Toad

Mexican Cone-nosed Toad

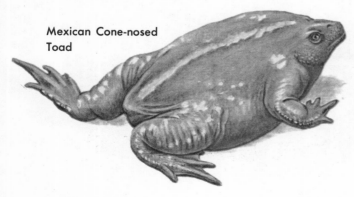

of its eggs much as the marsupial frogs do—but the males carry them. As the female lays her eggs, she winds the strings around the male's hind legs; she also piles them on his back. Wherever the male goes, he carries the eggs with him, until they hatch.

Even more unusual is the Surinam toad of northern South America. The male presses each egg into the thick, soft skin that develops on the female's back. Each egg then occupies its own nursery pouch. The young do not emerge until they are fully formed toadlets that can hop away on their own. Her maternity chore ended, the female rubs off the old thick skin. At best, however, a Surinam toad is grotesque. It has a wide, flat head and tiny, pinhead-sized eyes. Its legs and toes are long and skinny.

Unlike most other toads, the Surinam toad spends almost all of its life in water. The African clawed toad, so-called because of the clawlike tips on its toes, is also an aquatic toad. Neither of these toads has a tongue, which would be of no use to them in their watery homes.

When frightened or disturbed, the European fire-bellied toad lies on its stomach and bends its head and legs up over its body. This exposes its bright red underside, which is presumably a frightening or warning signal to attackers. The brightly colored Zetek's toad of the American tropics is very poisonous. If an attacker is not scared away by the colors, it may not live to regret its mistake.

Mexican cone-nosed toads have short legs, a small head, and an extremely large and flabby body. These burrowing toads feed mainly on ants and termites. Unlike the typical toads, their tongue is attached at the rear of the mouth.

Salamanders—Amphibians With Tails

Salamanders are amphibians with tails. The tail distinguishes them from frogs and toads. They are commonly confused with lizards, however, for these two kinds of animals do look much alike.

A salamander's skin is smooth and moist, like a frog's. A lizard, which is a reptile, has a scaly skin. The salamander has four toes or fewer on its front feet, and it has no claws. A lizard has five toes, which do bear claws.

All salamanders, which lack ears and do not make noises, as frogs and toads do, require moist surroundings. Some spend their entire lives in water. They are generally active only at night, hiding during the day in burrows or under rocks or logs.

Salamanders are more abundant in the cool, moist regions of North America than anywhere else in the world. Only a few kinds range into Central America and northern South America. Some occur in the temperate regions of Europe and Asia. Even fewer are found in northern Africa. Salamanders cannot tolerate great amounts of heat. None of them live in the tropics of South America, Africa, or Asia, and none are found in Australia or on nearby islands.

The giant salamander that lives in quiet pools and streams of China and Japan is a sluggish animal that reaches a length of five feet and may weigh as much as a hundred pounds. It is the largest of all living salamanders. There were prehistoric salamanders more than fifteen feet long.

Similar in habits and appearance is the hellbender, found in the Mississippi River and its tributaries. About eighteen inches long, with occasional individuals a bit larger, the hellbender is much more active than the giant salamander. It is an ugly animal—reddish brown, with a wrinkled skin. Night fishermen are sometimes startled to find a hellbender on their hook, for, like other members of the salamander

Giant Salamander

Congo Eel

Mud Puppy

Hellbender

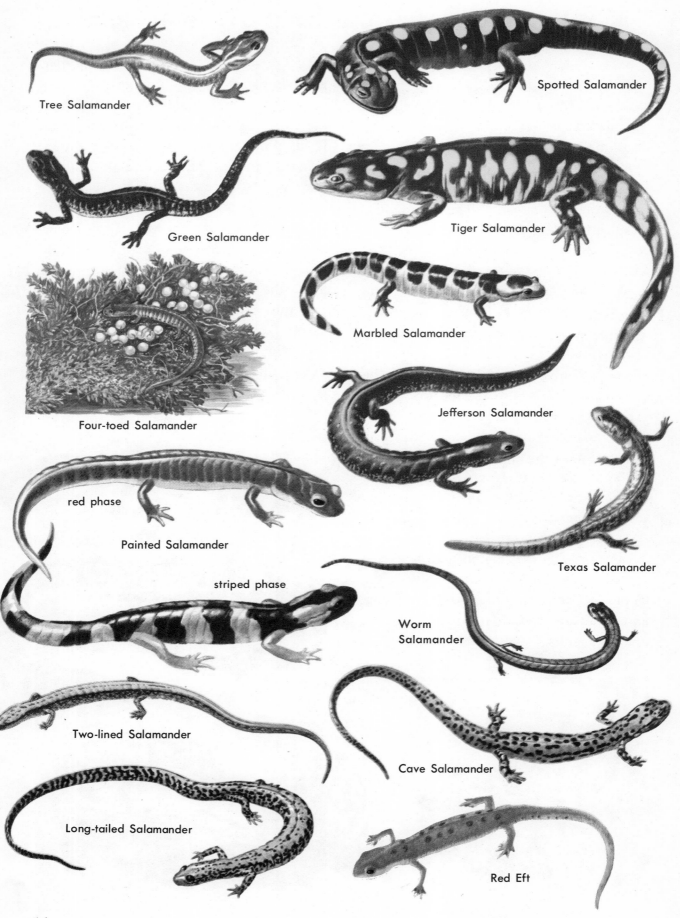

Tree Salamander

Spotted Salamander

Green Salamander

Tiger Salamander

Marbled Salamander

Four-toed Salamander

Jefferson Salamander

red phase

Painted Salamander

Texas Salamander

striped phase

Worm Salamander

Two-lined Salamander

Cave Salamander

Long-tailed Salamander

Red Eft

group, they prowl for food at night and are seldom seen during the day.

A more common large salamander is the mud puppy, or water dog, that lives in rivers and lakes of eastern North America. Mud puppies have conspicuous red, branched gills on each side of the head. They also have lungs, and, like most amphibians, they can breathe through their skin.

Congo eels, which may be more than three feet long, have tiny legs that are useless for walking. These snakelike salamanders bite viciously. They slither through the weedy waters of ponds and ditches in southern United States. Sirens, which inhabit the same region, have only front legs, and they keep their plumelike gills throughout their life.

Most salamanders are very small animals, few of them more than five inches long. One of the smallest is the four-toed salamander that averages only about two inches in length. It lives in northeastern United States. A close relative in southeastern United States is even smaller, sometimes less than an inch long.

Like frogs and toads, most salamanders lay their eggs in water. Some produce strings of eggs; others lay them in clumps; still others lay their eggs singly. A few kinds hold the eggs inside their body until they hatch and then give birth to miniature adults.

A salamander larva has legs and three feathery gills on each side of its head. Frog and toad tadpoles have only two gills on each side of the head, and by the time their legs appear, these gills are usually grown over with skin. In the typical salamanders, the larva loses its gills as it grows and changes into the adult stage that lives on land.

In the group of salamanders called newts, some have an extra stage in their life history. The eggs hatch into gilled larvae that change within a few months into warty-skinned, land-dwelling forms called efts. Efts never mature while living on land. After two or three years, an eft returns to the water and becomes an adult newt that lives out its life in the water.

One of the most commonly seen salamanders in eastern North America is the coral-colored red eft, which is the land-dwelling stage of the eastern newt. The adults are green with red spots and have broad tails for swimming. Newts are the most abundant kind of salamanders in European countries.

Among the strangest of all the salamanders are the blind, colorless kinds that live in caves. Their skin may be so thin that their blood and internal organs show through. Some live in artesian waters as much as a hundred feet below the surface. They are starved-looking animals—which indeed they are, for the water at those depths contains almost no food. These unusual salamanders survive by absorbing nutrition directly from the water, taking in none by mouth.

Blind Salamanders

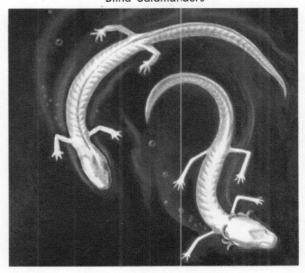

Turtles—Living Tanks

Turtles have shells. This fact sets them apart from all other reptiles. A turtle's upper shell is called the carapace. The lower shell is called the plastron. In some kinds of turtles, the lower shell is almost as thick and hard as the upper shell; in others, it is thin and flexible. These two halves of the shell are joined at the edges, with spaces for the head, tail, and legs to stick out. These exposed parts of the body are protected by a scaly covering, as in snakes and lizards. Some kinds of turtles can close their shells completely, drawing their legs, head, and tail out of sight. Others do not have this protection; usually these are the kinds that can bite.

Turtles do not have teeth. Instead, they have a horny beak, the edges of which are very sharp. In some, the edges are saw-toothed, so they serve as teeth for tearing food into chunks. Because they have powerful jaws, turtles can give dangerous bites. Some kinds will not let loose once their jaws snap shut. Others are extremely gentle and never bite.

All turtles lay eggs. Most turtles make a crude nest in decaying vegetation or dig in loose dirt or sand to bury their eggs. The eggs of some are round and white,

Painted Turtle

looking much like small Ping-Pong balls. Others are oblong. The shells are tough and leathery. Some turtles lay only a few eggs; others lay several hundred. After her eggs are laid, the female leaves the nest. When the eggs hatch, the young turtles must care for themselves.

The typical turtles have flipperlike feet for swimming. They live mostly in water. Terrapins are web-footed turtles that

Life History of Slider Turtle

spend part of their time in water and part on land. Tortoises, which have a high, domelike shell and stumpy legs, are land-dwelling turtles.

Sliders are common turtles of southern United States. One reason they are so well known is that sliders are the kind most often kept as pets. Turtles do make interesting pets, and their demands are not great. They do not display affection as warm-blooded animals do, but they learn to come for food when signaled, and they like to be stroked. If well cared for, they will live for a long time.

Recently, however, pet turtles have been suspected of carrying a disease, so it might be well to wait for the results of the investigations before keeping one.

Painted turtles are similar to the sliders but are more widely distributed, occurring also in western United States. The margin of their shells is smooth at the rear, not scalloped as sliders' shells are. The edge of the upper shell is patterned with red, both top and underside, and the yellowish lower shell is also attractively marked with red. The amount of this color varies with the kinds of painted turtle and from one region to another.

The long-necked chicken turtle of extreme southeastern United States is prized there for food; its flesh tastes much like chicken. It often lives in the same waters as sliders, but it has a mean disposition and does not make a good pet. Other common turtles of the same general region are the musk and mud turtles. Both give off a strong odor—musky, or swamplike, rich with the smell of the muck in which they live.

The Pacific turtle, the only common freshwater turtle of the West, lives in lakes and streams along the coast, from Canada southward to Mexico. It is closely related to the common spotted turtle of eastern United States, but it is slightly larger and has less distinct spots on its upper shell.

Snappers are quick-tempered, vicious turtles that will strike like a snake at an intruder. They have long necks, and the edges of their jaws are sharp. Snappers can strike from a surprising distance, so they must be treated with caution.

The common snapper lives in ponds, lakes, and some streams throughout eastern United States and westward to the Rocky Mountains. It averages less than five pounds in weight. There are reports now and then of common snappers weighing fifteen or twenty pounds being caught. The record is forty-five pounds.

Common Snapper

Saw-toothed Slider

Blanding Turtle

Pacific Turtle

Alligator Snapper

Eastern Painted Turtle

Chicken Turtle

Common Musk Turtle

Elegant Slider

male

female

young

Mud Turtle

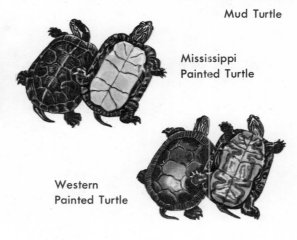

Mississippi
Painted Turtle

Western
Painted Turtle

Midland Painted Turtle

19

The alligator snapper, found only in extreme southern United States, is the largest of the snappers and one of the largest of all turtles. It weighs more than a hundred pounds. Compared to the active and aggressive common snapper, the alligator snapper is a sluggish animal. With its mouth gaping open, it lies on the bottom in quiet waters. A wormlike projection on its tongue stands up, wriggling with the slightest movement of the water. Fish are attracted to this lure, and when they make a dash to get this meal, they must enter the turtle's mouth. The turtle's jaws snap shut, and the fish is quickly gulped down.

The soft-shelled turtles have leathery, flexible shells. A soft-shell can draw in its feet and head, but the soft shell provides almost no protection. Soft-shells make up for this lack by being fast swimmers, and if they are not able to escape, they fight. They have long, snakelike necks that permit them to bite at an enemy almost directly behind them. They strike with astonishing speed.

Normally, the soft-shelled turtles' long necks and speed are useful to them in getting the fish, frogs, and other animals that they eat. The long neck also serves as a sort of snorkel when the turtles bury themselves in the sand in shallow water. A buried turtle can stretch its long neck up through the sand and all the way to the surface of the water to breathe. At the slightest disturbance, it pulls its neck back into the sand and out of sight.

Soft-shells are prized as food. A turtle hunter soon learns how to recognize the place a soft-shell is buried. A funnel-shaped depression marks the exact spot where a turtle has withdrawn its head. Carefully, judging the size of the turtle by the size of the funnel, the turtle hunter slides his hands down into the sand and grabs the turtle by each side of its shell. Quickly he pulls the creature out. No matter where it is held, the soft-shell might reach back and give a severe bite, so the turtle hunter drops his catch into some safe container immediately.

Soft-shells are so completely aquatic that they rarely come out of water except to bask on the shore. Their feet are

Soft-shelled Turtle

Snake-necked Turtle

broadly webbed for swimming. The females lay their eggs in sand at the water's edge, and the newly hatched turtles do not have far to travel to get into water. Soft-shells average only two to four pounds in weight, but occasional individuals may weigh fifteen to twenty pounds.

Among the strangest of all the aquatic freshwater turtles are the snake-necked turtles of Australia and the closely related matamatas of South America. These turtles have exceptionally long necks, which they withdraw sideways so that they fit in front of their legs. Most turtles draw their necks straight in and crook them into an *S* shape vertically. The three-foot matamata lives in the silted, muddy waters of the Amazon and its tributaries. It has

feelerlike bits of skin hanging from its neck and lower jaw. These presumably look like worms to the small fishes that swim closer. The turtle opens its huge, weak-jawed mouth and, at the same time, expands its throat. This causes water to rush in to fill these cavities. The little fish are literally sucked in by the sudden swift flow of water.

All of the several closely related snake-necked turtles of South America are almost strictly aquatic, coming to land only to lay eggs. The Australian snake-necked turtle is at home both on land and in water. This is a small turtle, only about ten inches long, and its fully extended neck does indeed look like a snake emerging from the shell.

Matamata

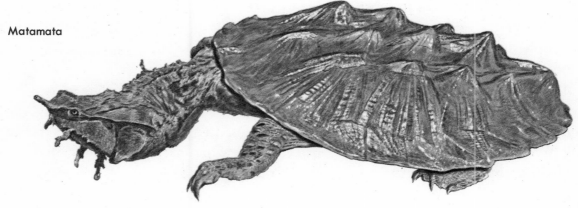

Wood Turtle

Box Turtle

Land-dwelling Turtles

Box turtles are found east of the Rockies, from southern Canada southward throughout the United States. When food is plentiful, box turtles will eat so much that they can no longer get completely inside their shell. Like other tortoises, they eat mainly plants.

Box turtles are about six inches long and can bury themselves in loose dirt or leaves to hide. But they usually escape by simply tucking their head and legs inside their shell and then closing it tightly. No amount of thumping or prying can force it open. The timid turtle stays inside as long as there is a commotion. When all is quiet, the turtle opens its shell slightly and peeks out. If all appears safe, it sticks out its legs and goes on its way again.

The wood turtle, a small land-dwelling turtle that lives in northeastern United States, has two prominent ridges, or keels, down the middle of the upper shell. During dry weather, this tortoise moves to swampy lowlands or to streams and ponds, but when the woods are moist, it stays away from water. Unlike the box turtles, it cannot withdraw completely into its shell.

Gopher turtles that live in desert regions are the master burrowers among turtles. In their underground hideaways, they escape the dry, hot days, then come out during the night to munch on plants.

Besides having stumpy, powerful legs, similar to those of other tortoises, the gophers have a trowel-shaped extension on the front of their lower shell. This serves as a sort of plow when the animal is pushing loose dirt from its burrow, which may be thirty feet long and as much as ten feet below the surface.

Early explorers found huge land-dwelling turtles, or tortoises, living in countless numbers on the rocky Galapagos Islands off the western coast of South America. They sampled them as food and discovered that their flavor was superb. Soon the islands became a regular stop for explorers, whalers, and fishermen, who regarded the giant tortoise as a staple in their ships' larders.

It is estimated that more than 10 million giant tortoises were hauled away from the islands by seafarers. Laws now prevent the removal of those few that have survived.

Compared to other tortoises, the giant tortoise of the Galapagos Islands is indeed the mightiest. Its high-arched shell may be as much as four feet long and almost as tall. It may weigh nearly five hundred pounds. Despite its size, this giant is gentle, no more dangerous than the smallest of the box turtles. Those kept in zoos and other wildlife exhibits become lumbering rides for children.

A persistent myth about all turtles, and particularly the tortoises, is that they live for many centuries. It is true that they may live for as long as one hundred fifty years or even a bit longer, but it is most surprising that they reach their maximum size in so short a time. A giant tortoise only fifteen years old, for example, may weigh over four hundred pounds.

All of the several kinds of large tortoises live in warm or tropical regions. Those that live in cool climates are much smaller. They survive the winters by hibernating—in burrows or buried in the soil or in litter.

Gopher Turtle

Giant Tortoise

Sea Turtles—Giants of the Turtle World

Sea turtles live in warm seas throughout the world. They never come to shore except to lay their eggs.

When spring tides are highest, the female drags her heavy body up the beach. Her legs are flippers, excellent for swimming but almost useless for walking on land. If she is unable to select a good place the first time, she must labor her way back to the sea and then try again another time.

She must find a place that is sandy so that the digging is easy. It must also be just above the high tide mark so that the eggs will not be soaked with salt water. When she finds the right spot, the female digs a hole. In this hole, she lays her eggs—ten or twelve dozen, about the size of duck eggs but round and with rubbery shells. Her task completed, the female shoves sand into the hole and crawls back to the sea.

The warm sun incubates the eggs buried in the sand. In about a month,

they hatch, and the dozens of tiny sea turtles struggle to the surface and begin scrambling toward the sea. This is a dangerous time for the little turtles, for they are the right-sized morsels for gulls and other creatures that search the beaches for food. For hours, even after they are in the sea, the little turtles are not safe. Still carrying food from the yolk in their bodies, they bob about like corks until this food is used up. Then they become full-fledged creatures of the sea.

The heaviest of all living reptiles is the leatherback, or trunkback, turtle, which may be six feet long or longer and weigh as much as fifteen hundred pounds. The leatherback does not have a shell. Instead, its armor consists of thick ridges that run lengthwise down its back. These are filled with blubber several inches thick. The ridges and the spaces between are covered with a thick, leathery skin.

All of the other sea turtles have typical shells. Loggerhead and green turtles grow to a very large size—four hundred pounds or more. A hawksbill is smaller, seldom weighing more than a hundred pounds. It is famous as the source of genuine tortoiseshell, made from the polished horny plates of its shell. Both loggerhead and green turtles are eaten,

but the green turtle is much favored because of its flavor, which is like veal. The green turtle grazes on plants that grow in warm, shallow seas. The loggerhead's diet of fish, jellyfish, and other sea animals gives its flesh a stronger flavor.

Green turtles got their name from the bluish green color of their fat, which is prized for soup. At one time, vast numbers of these turtles were harvested in Caribbean waters. When they began to be scarce, it was feared that they might become extinct. Efforts to save them may have come just in time—or hopefully so. Most countries that harvest green turtles now cooperate in trying to assure a continued supply in the future.

Green turtles were fished for by the natives of the Caribbean islands long before the arrival of European explorers. On his second voyage, Columbus saw the unusual way the turtles were caught at sea. When a turtle was sighted basking at the surface, a fisherman moved his canoe as close as he could without scaring it. Then he let over the side a remora, or suckerfish, tied to a strong line. The remora headed for the turtle—the nearest large object to which it could attach itself. As soon as the remora was securely fastened to the turtle, the fisherman began working the turtle toward shallow water, where it could be roped and taken ashore.

Leatherback Turtle

Loggerhead Turtle

Green Turtle

Hawksbill Turtle

25

Frilled Lizard

Lizards—Desert Dwellers

Lizards have legs. Snakes do not. This is the most obvious difference between these two groups of reptiles. But a few kinds of lizards are legless, too. All lizards, however, have small external ear openings—holes at the sides of their head—and they have movable eyelids. Snakes do not have either. Also, lizards do not have an elastic ligament connecting the two halves of their lower jaw. Snakes do, enabling them to stretch their mouth over prey several times larger around than themselves. The scales on a lizard's belly are much like those on its back. On a snake's belly is a single row of plates running the length of the body.

Like most reptiles, lizards lay eggs. The few kinds that live in cold climates hold their eggs inside their body until they hatch, then give birth to their fully developed young.

Because of its legs, a lizard's tail is set off distinctly from its body, while it is difficult to tell at a glance exactly where a snake's tail begins. The tail is the part of a lizard's body that is usually grabbed by a predator. In many kinds, the tail pops off the body if touched or if the lizard becomes sufficiently excited. While the shed tail, wormlike and enticing, continues to wiggle and keep the attacker's attention, the lizard itself goes off

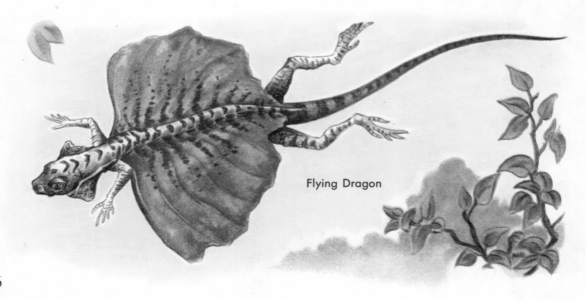

Flying Dragon

into hiding. A new tail will grow to replace the old one. The new one is generally shorter and also lacks a bony extension from the backbone.

Gila monsters, chuckwallas, and other lizards that live in dry regions have fat, stubby tails in which they store food. This tides them over during the times when their hunting goes poorly. Swift-running lizards that use only their extra-long hind legs have very long tails that serve as balancers.

over them and makes "wings" that enable the lizard to glide for long distances—from branch to branch or from the top of a tree to a soft landing on the ground.

As in snakes, a lizard's tongue is one of its most important sensory organs. It is used to sample the surroundings and may be flicked in and out of the mouth regularly. Of all the lizards, chameleons have the most specialized tongues. They may be longer than the lizard's body.

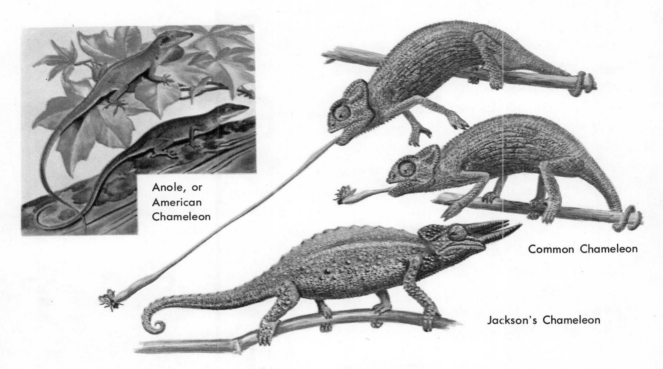

Anole, or American Chameleon

Common Chameleon

Jackson's Chameleon

The frilled lizard of Australia has folds of loose skin on its neck. When disturbed, the lizard stretches this skin into a huge, frilly collar that is brightly colored inside. At the same time, it opens its mouth wide to show the gaudy inside lining. Bright colors, especially when flashed suddenly, are generally frightening to other animals.

The flying dragon is an Asiatic lizard that has loose folds of skin along the sides of its body. When it lifts its extra-long ribs, this skin stretches tightly

Chameleons are best known for their ability to change colors to match their surroundings. They can shift from gray to green or to mottled shades in between. The eyes of these African lizards are in turretlike bulges. Each eye can be moved independently of the other. When a chameleon spies an insect, it moves, slowly and cautiously, close enough that the insect can be reached with its sticky-tipped tongue. The long tongue shoots out of the chameleon's mouth and back in again so rapidly that the eye cannot follow the movement. But the insect has disappeared!

Anoles, or American chameleons, common in Florida and the American subtropics, are not related to the true chameleons. They are called chameleons only because they can change their color from gray to green or brown. In mating season, the males puff out discs of brightly colored skin on their throats.

In the United States, lizards are most abundant in the dry western states. Snakes are more common in the moister eastern part of the country. Most of the desert-dwelling lizards, which include the utas, whiptail lizards, and sand lizards, can run swiftly. Some have fringes on their toes that help them in scampering over the sand without sinking in. This is important in dashing over the hot sand from one spot of shade to another and in escaping predators in the wide-open spaces, where hiding is difficult.

Exceptions are the horned lizards (often called horned toads) that are so squat that they do not even cast a shadow. Their toadlike bodies are covered with short spines that also form formidable crowns atop their heads.

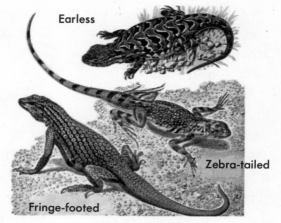

Earless

Zebra-tailed

Fringe-footed

Sand Lizards

Six-lined

Tiger

Whiptail Lizards

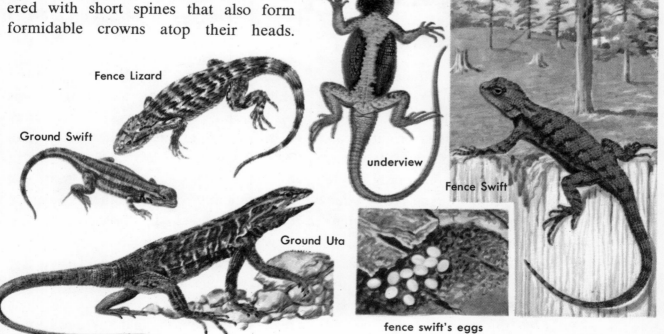

Fence Lizard

Ground Swift

Ground Uta

underview

Fence Swift

fence swift's eggs

28

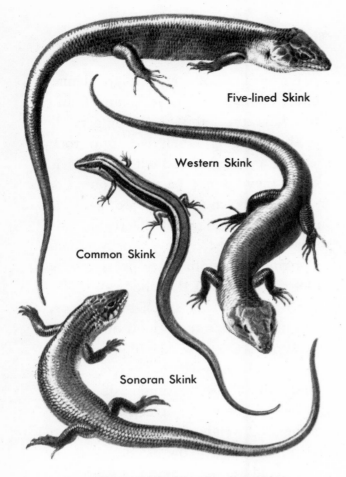

Five-lined Skink

Western Skink

Common Skink

Sonoran Skink

eggs underground

Horned Lizard

Gila Monster

Though normally they move sluggishly, horned lizards can also run with great speed. If cornered, they hiss, bulge their eyes, and attack. When angered, they sometimes squirt drops of blood from their eyes.

The fat-tailed, poisonous Gila monsters, the only venomous lizards in the world, are also desert-dwellers. One of the two kinds lives in Mexico and southwestern United States; the other is found only in Mexico. Their venom, which affects the nervous system, is one of the most potent in the reptile world. Fortunately, the lizards have poorly developed fangs for injecting the poison, and their bite wounds bleed so profusely that the venom is usually flushed away. A Gila monster's body is covered with hard, beadlike bumps rather than with the usual flat scales.

Only two kinds of lizards—skinks and spiny swifts—are common in eastern United States north of Florida. Skinks are ground-dwellers that live in fallen, rotting logs or in the decaying hollows of trees. Their young have blue tails that are shed easily. Swifts are fleet little lizards that race over the ground like the desert utas. Both belong to the same large family of lizards, the iguanas, which includes some of the largest of all the lizards.

Two kinds of iguanas share the rocky Galapagos Islands with the giant tortoises. One is the marine iguana, which may be more than four feet long. Though it looks like a sullen, ferocious beast, this big lizard is really quite docile. Groups of these iguanas loll on the rocks, always at the edge of the sea. From time to time, they dive into the water to forage for seaweed. They are

Komodo Dragon

They get their water from the cactus plants they eat.

Chuckwallas, of southwestern United States, also belong to the iguana family. They have the habit of escaping predators by wedging themselves into rocky crevices and inflating their bodies with air, so they cannot be pulled out. Like most iguanas, chuckwallas are good eating, and the Indians of the region used to retrieve them from their rocky retreats by poking them with sharp-pointed sticks to let the air out of their bodies.

The largest of all the lizards are several kinds of monitors found only in the Old World. Of these, the biggest is the Komodo dragon, which lives on a few islands off the tip of southeastern Asia. Komodo dragons may reach a length of ten feet and weigh as much as three hundred fifty pounds. Now listed among the endangered animals, these big lizards are usually wary and difficult to approach. In search of food, a Komodo dragon may attack deer or wild hogs.

strong swimmers, but they can also walk along the bottom, using their powerful claws to cling to the rocks. The smaller, three-foot land iguanas are not mild-mannered and will make rushing attacks if approached too closely. Land iguanas live in the dry interior of the islands.

Marine Iguana

Common Iguana

Black Iguana

Land Iguana

Chuckwalla

Bull Snake

Snakes—Legless Reptiles

Few people have a kind word for snakes. Most legends depict them as villainous animals. True, snakes do slither, being legless creatures; and because they lack eyelids, they do have an unblinking stare that can be disturbing. Some are extremely poisonous. But it is also true that most kinds are harmless, and many are importantly helpful in the control of rats, mice, and other pests.

Most of the roughly 2,700 kinds of snakes (slightly fewer than lizards) live in the tropics. As a group, snakes prefer moister surroundings than do lizards.

Pine Snake

Many live in temperate regions, however, and one kind, the European viper, ranges even into the Arctic Circle. Iceland, Antarctica, and Ireland are the only large land areas that have no snakes at all.

As with lizards, there are some big bluffers among the snakes. When a bull snake, found in western United States, is come upon suddenly, it coils, hisses, and vibrates its tail rapidly. If the tail strikes dry leaves, the sound is much like the rattling of a rattlesnake. A bull snake will bite if it is picked up, as most snakes will, but the bite is not harmful. In striking and then drawing back, a snake's numerous small teeth may tear the skin, but they are too short to penetrate deeply. The only danger is an infection in the wound.

Bull snakes and their close relatives, the pine snakes of southern United States, are among the most valuable of all snakes, for they make most of their meals of rats and mice. They are constrictors, killing their prey by crushing and suffocating it in their body coils. Snakes are especially effective against rodents, because snakes are slender enough to enter a burrow and destroy the young in a nest.

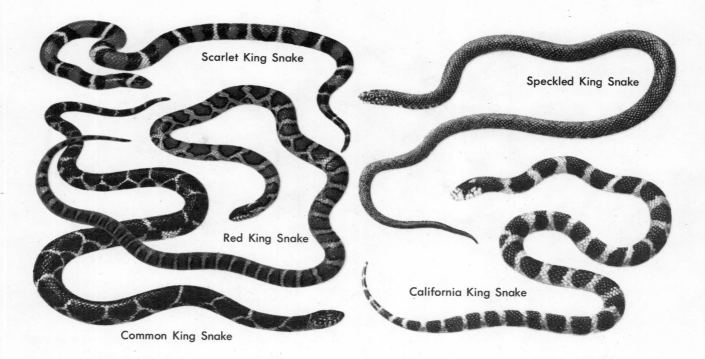

Scarlet King Snake

Speckled King Snake

Red King Snake

California King Snake

Common King Snake

The hognose snakes, or puffing adders, of North America are surely the champion bluffers of the snake world. When a hognose snake is cornered, it flattens its body by extending its ribs, hisses noisily, and strikes. But, interestingly, it does not even open its mouth when it strikes! If these sinister acts do not scare away an intruder, the snake tries another performance. It rolls onto its back, opens its mouth, and lets its tongue hang out. It writhes for several minutes, as though dying. Then it becomes very quiet, looking for all the world as though it were dead. But it does insist that a dead snake must lie on its back. If you turn it onto its stomach, it quickly rolls onto its back again! If it is left alone, it will, in time, lift its head and look around to see whether all is safe. Satisfied that it will not be bothered, it rolls onto its stomach and crawls away. In captivity, hognose snakes will refuse to repeat these performances after doing their act several times.

Hognose snakes have upturned snouts, like hogs, or pigs, which explains their name. They use these hard snouts to push into loose soil. They eat only cold-blooded animals, such as insects, frogs, toads, and salamanders.

Among the most attractive of the North American snakes are the several kinds of king snakes. The scarlet king snake mimics the poisonous coral snake, but it has a red nose, and the yellow bands have a black band on each side. In North American coral snakes, the nose is black, and

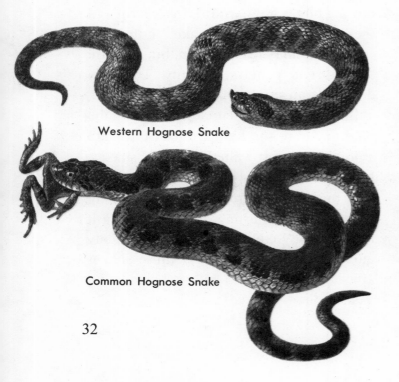

Western Hognose Snake

Common Hognose Snake

the black bands have a yellow band on each side.

King snakes are best known for their habit of eating other snakes. They do not make it their business to find rattlesnakes, as many believe, but they do not shy away from them. Incredibly, a rattlesnake that is being attacked by a king snake seems to resort to biting only when all other attempts to escape have failed. Even then, the king snake is not killed by the rattlesnake's venom. King snakes overcome their victims by constriction. A snake is difficult to kill in this manner, however, so the king snake usually swallows its victim while it is still alive. King snakes also eat insects, birds, and mammals. They are highly valued for controlling rodents.

Rat snakes, which include the fox snake and corn snake, are another group of North American harmless snakes with a good reputation for eating rodents. Most of the several kinds are marked with colorful blotches. The yellow rat snake is striped with black, and the black rat

Western Racer

Eastern Racer

snake, which also goes by the name of pilot black snake, is black with red and yellow tips on its scales. Rat snakes will coil and strike when first approached.

The several kinds of whip snakes and racers are among the speediest of all snakes. Speed in snakes is generally exaggerated, however. It is probable that no

Fox Snake

Corn Snake

Common Garter Snake

Plains Garter Snake

Western Garter Snake

the world. Those in North America are all harmless, but some of their relatives in other countries are poisonous. Like most snakes, they lay eggs.

Garter snakes give birth to their young. The female holds the eggs inside her body until they hatch. Most females give birth to only a dozen or two young at a time, but there are records of female garter snakes giving birth to as many as seventy! All of the garter snakes, except one blotched Mexican species, are striped with yellow. The spaces between are dark in some and light in others. Some kinds are always found near water.

snake travels more than eight to ten miles per hour—and most of them only about half this fast. Their quick, dodging turns make them appear to be going faster and also make them more difficult to catch.

When a snake is in a hurry, it wiggles its body rapidly in a series of *S* shapes. When it is not in a hurry, a snake moves in almost a straight line. It presses its body tightly against the ground, using the plates on its belly for traction so that it flows along smoothly.

Racers and whip snakes are nervous snakes. They do not tame easily. They belong to one of the largest families of snakes, with representatives throughout

Common Water Snake

Painted Water Snake

34

Others live only in dry upland regions. Most garter snakes give off a strong musky odor when first caught.

Of all the snakes, the kinds that live in water are among the best known, possibly because they are more easily seen. They spend a portion of their time basking in the sun along the shore. Like garter snakes, they bear their young alive. Most kinds have vicious tempers and need little encouragement to bite. They are not poisonous. (Water moccasins are water-dwelling venomous snakes but of a different family—the vipers.) They eat small fish, frogs, and other animals caught in or near the water. Excellent swimmers, they can remain submerged for long periods of time. DeKay's snake and the red-bellied snake are two common water snakes of eastern United States, but they are so secretive that they are seldom seen. The line snake, found in the same general region, is rare.

Snakes have small scales on their back and large plates over their belly. As the

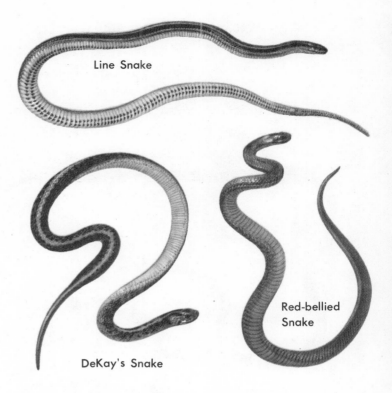

Line Snake

DeKay's Snake

Red-bellied Snake

snake grows, the skin over these scales is shed. If a snake is eating regularly, it may shed its skin several times a year. Just before the snake sheds, the transparent covering over its eyes becomes milky, and for a few days, the snake is nearly blind. Meanwhile, its colors become dull as the skin pulls away from the scales. When the time is right, the snake rubs its nose against a rock, tree root, or some other rough or sharp object to pull the skin loose from the end of its nose. Then it simply crawls out of the old skin, which turns inside out.

Most snakes have small teeth that curve backward. This prevents prey that is being swallowed alive from squirming out. The only direction they can move is forward, on into the snake's stomach. A snake swallows an animal headfirst. If it should make a mistake and try to swallow an animal tailfirst, which sometimes happens, it often cannot manage a stretched-out leg, because the leg will not bend forward.

Green Water Snake

Diamond-backed Water Snake

A snake can swallow an animal several times its own size, however. This is possible because the snake can separate its lower jaw from its upper jaw to make its mouth much wider. Snakes have been known to enter cages and swallow animals so large that they could not get back through the bars afterward.

The swallowing process is slow. If the prey is very large, it may require several hours for the snake to get its meal out of sight, and even longer before the meal is digested. A snake's digestive juices are powerful, for they must digest unchewed

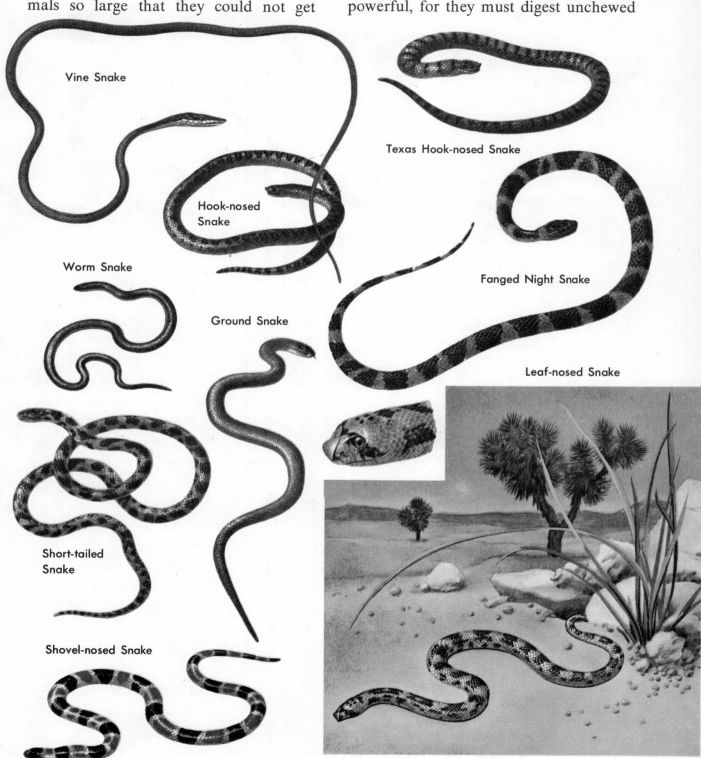

Vine Snake

Texas Hook-nosed Snake

Hook-nosed Snake

Worm Snake

Ground Snake

Fanged Night Snake

Leaf-nosed Snake

Short-tailed Snake

Shovel-nosed Snake

food. Even bones and shells are dissolved during digestion.

Some kinds of snakes are rare and not often seen. Others live in swampy or muddy areas or similar places where people seldom travel. The snakes on these pages—from the vine snake to the sand snake—are mostly less familiar kinds. Some of these kinds are indeed interesting in their ways of life. The long, narrow-headed vine snake, for example, is limited to Mexico and a small area of the American Southwest, where it lives in shrubs. Leaf-nosed snakes are desert dwellers of the Southwest, the thick shield over their nose aiding them in

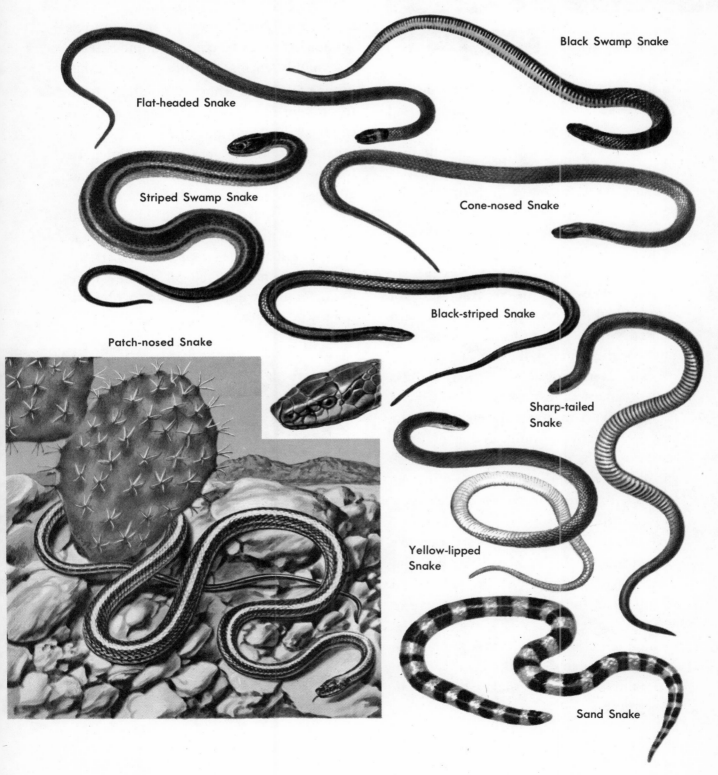

Black Swamp Snake

Flat-headed Snake

Striped Swamp Snake

Cone-nosed Snake

Black-striped Snake

Patch-nosed Snake

Sharp-tailed Snake

Yellow-lipped Snake

Sand Snake

Ring-necked Snake

pushing through the sand. Hook-nosed, patch-nosed, sand, and shovel-nosed snakes are also sand burrowers.

Worm snakes, widely distributed in southeastern United States, are burrowers that rarely come to the surface. Also seldom seen, though locally abundant, are ground, short-tailed, sharp-tailed, yellow-lipped, and black-striped snakes.

Among the most attractive of the secretive snakes are the several kinds of ring-necked snakes that live in eastern United States. They usually keep well out of sight, under fallen logs or rocks or in leaf litter and debris. Their back is gray to black, and just behind the head is a yellowish orange ring encircling the neck. The belly is orange red, sometimes marked with dark spots. When these snakes are exposed, they typically turn so that this bright color shows as a warning to the intruder.

Common, but difficult to see because of their camouflaging color, are the slim green snakes that live in vines and shrubs or in tall grass. Two kinds live in eastern United States. One has scales with smooth surfaces; in the other, each scale has a ridge down the center. Green is a common color of snakes that live in trees and vines.

Snakes spend most of the day sunning or resting, moving about most actively and feeding at night. They are generally so inconspicuous that they may go unnoticed, even if they are common in an area. Just a casual walk may reveal no snakes at all, while a careful search, in which rocks and logs are overturned, may produce a surprising number.

As a group, snakes fit into nature's scheme as valuable control animals, feeding mainly on insects, rodents, and other kinds of animals whose populations need to be kept in balance. The temptation to catch snakes and put them in cages is great, but few of them make good pets, for they do not respond to petting and affection as many other pets do. Worse, they are too often neglected when caged. They may be poorly fed or get infestations of mites under their scales. Certainly, they are not as well off as they were living in the wild. It is best to observe snakes in nature, where they belong.

Keeled Green Snake

keeled scale

Green Snake

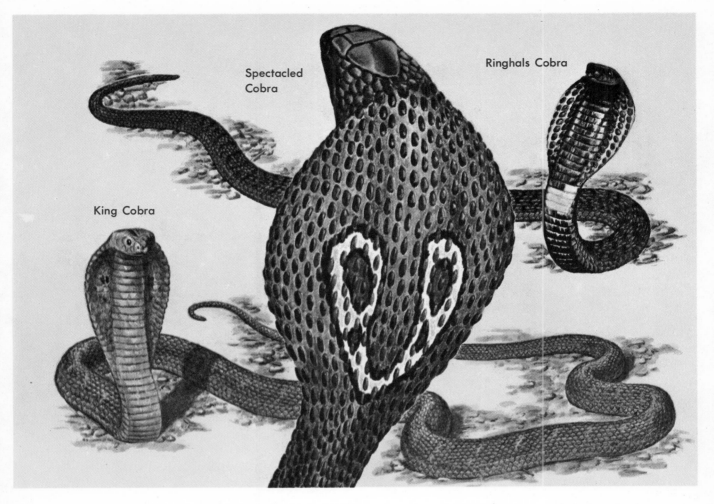

Spectacled Cobra

Ringhals Cobra

King Cobra

Snakes to Beware Of

The largest of all the poisonous snakes in the world is the king cobra of southern Asia. It averages eight to ten feet in length but is known to reach a length of eighteen feet. One of these giants contains enough venom to kill an elephant in only seconds. The poison affects the nervous system, paralyzing the centers that control the victim's breathing.

The king cobra is one of the few snakes that feed almost exclusively on other snakes. Other kinds of cobras and their relatives eat mainly rodents. When a king cobra is disturbed, it lifts the long, thin ribs in its neck region and stretches the loose skin of its neck over them. This makes the hood for which this snake is so famous. The female king cobra is unusual among snakes because she protects her eggs.

Some other kinds of cobras can spread a hood; some cannot. The back of the hood of the spectacled cobra bears two black and white marks. Legend has it that these are the finger marks of Buddha, who put his fingers there to bless the snake for shading his eyes with its hood while he was resting.

A snake charmer keeps his cobra in a basket and supposedly lures the snake out with the sound of music. The snake rises slowly and sways as the snake charmer plays. But the snake cannot hear music! It comes out because the lid has been

Common Coral Snake

Arizona Coral Snake

Death Adder

Tiger Snake

Black Snake

removed and the basket jiggled to disturb it. It sways in following the movements of the snake charmer's body.

Among the more than half a dozen kinds of cobras in Africa, the most famous is the Egyptian cobra, or asp. This is the snake believed to have been used by Cleopatra to commit suicide. Some of the African cobras can "spit" their venom accurately for ten feet or more. It can cause blindness if it strikes the eyes.

Closely related to cobras are the slim, tree-dwelling mambas of Africa. These swift, highly poisonous snakes are normally shy and will shun people. Occasionally, an angered mamba attacks when someone gets too close.

More than three dozen kinds of coral snakes are found mainly in South and Central America, and two kinds live in southern and southwestern United States. Closely related to cobras and mambas, these snakes are usually shy and secretive. This is fortunate, for their venom is very potent. Those found in the United States are small, rarely more than

Sea Snake

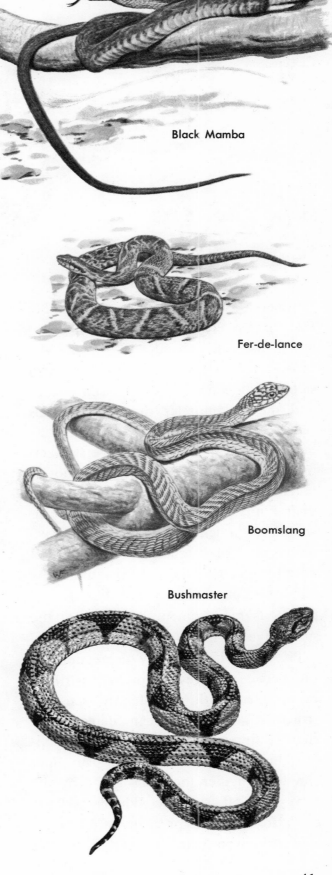

Black Mamba

Fer-de-lance

Boomslang

Bushmaster

eighteen inches long. A coral snake that lives in Brazil grows to five feet long.

Most of the snakes of Australia, where about eighty percent of all the snakes are poisonous, belong to the same group as coral snakes and cobras. Drop for drop, the six-foot Australian tiger snake has one of the most potent venoms of all the snakes in the world. Other common venomous Australian snakes are the death adder, which looks like a viper but is a cobra relative, and the black snake, which can spread a hood.

About fifty different kinds of sea snakes live in the Indian and Pacific oceans. Sea snakes sometimes appear in almost unbelievable numbers—literally millions. Some are as much as eight feet long. Many are attractively marked, with black above and yellow below. Some are spotted. A sea snake's nostrils are equipped with valves, and the upper jaw fits tightly over the lower jaw, like a lid. These keep out water when the snake submerges. Sea snakes must come to the surface from time to time to breathe air, but they can stay submerged for hours.

The venom of sea snakes is about as potent as the poison of cobras, their relatives. Because they are abundant, they are frequently caught in fishermen's nets. They also show up along bathing beaches, so it is astonishing that they cause so few deaths. Fortunately, they are reluctant to bite.

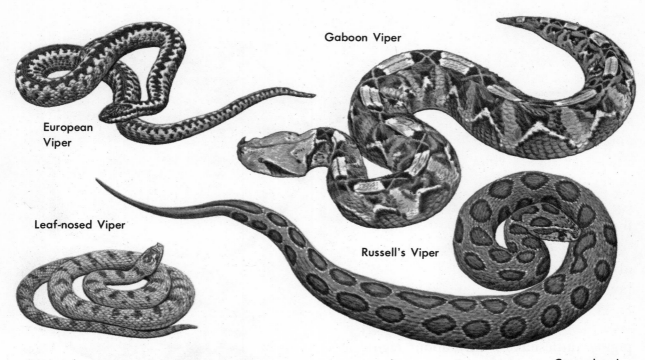

Gaboon Viper

European Viper

Leaf-nosed Viper

Russell's Viper

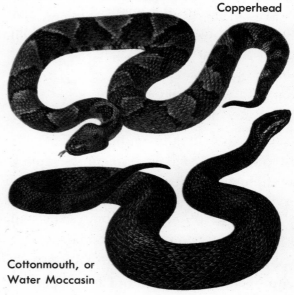

Copperhead

Cottonmouth, or Water Moccasin

Vipers have long, movable fangs that **fold against the roof of the mouth when** not in use. Their head is triangular, the broad rear portion marking, on each side, the location of the poison glands and the big muscles that squeeze this venom out through the hypodermiclike fangs. The venom of most vipers affects the blood and blood vessels. It is not as potent as the venom of the cobras and their kin, but large vipers produce their venom in much greater quantity. Russell's viper, of southeastern Asia, is believed to cause more deaths than any other poisonous snake—not because its poison is more potent but because the snake lives in heavily populated areas.

Pit vipers have a tiny depression, or pit, between the eye and the nostril on each side. With this highly sensitive structure, the snake can detect even slight differences in temperature. Without going into a rat's burrow, a pit viper can tell whether the rat is there by the heat given off from the rodent's body. It can also detect the presence of a bird on a branch, even in pitch-darkness.

The bushmaster, of the American tropics and subtropics, is the largest of the pit vipers. A vicious snake, it may reach a length of twelve feet. The fer-de-lance, found in the same region, has an equally mean disposition. It attains a length of about eight feet.

The South African boomslang is unusual in having its fangs at the rear of its mouth. Because it seldom tries to bite, the boomslang is not feared. It has caused many deaths, however.

The pitless, or true, vipers are Old World snakes. The European viper is a member of this group. Also included is the ugly, six-foot gaboon viper of Africa, with its head as wide as a man's hand and its fat and stubby body.

The leaf-nosed viper of northern India is one of several kinds of vipers that inhabit desert regions. The leaflike appendage on their nose helps prevent sand from entering their nostrils.

Rattlesnakes, of which there are more than three dozen species, are also pit vipers. Fifteen different kinds live in the United States. They range in size from pigmy rattlesnakes, only about eighteen inches long, to the giant Florida diamondback that may be eight feet long and as big around as a man's arm. Most of the rattlesnakes live in warm regions, but the timber and prairie rattlesnakes are found as far north as southern Canada.

A rattlesnake's rattle is made of a series of horny buttons attached at the tip of the tail. Each time the snake sheds its skin, it gets a new button. When the snake is disturbed, it vibrates its tail, and the buttons make a buzzing noise.

Other pit vipers in North America include the cottonmouth, or water moccasin, and the copperhead. The inside of a cottonmouth's mouth is literally as white as cotton, and the copperhead does indeed have a shiny, copper-colored head and coppery patches over its body. Neither is as poisonous as rattlesnakes.

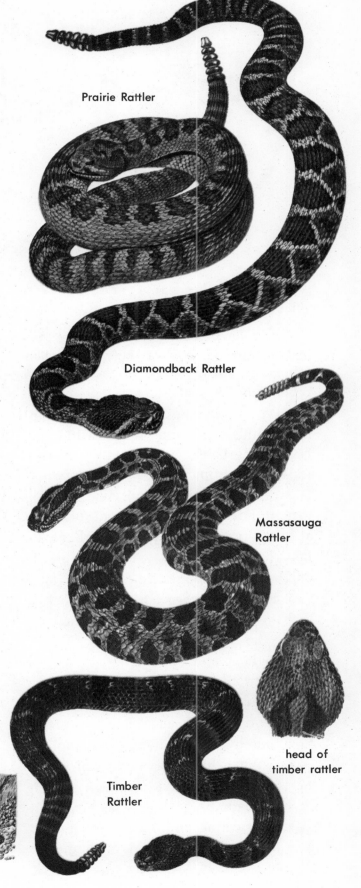

Prairie Rattler

Diamondback Rattler

Massasauga Rattler

head of timber rattler

Timber Rattler

Pigmy Rattler

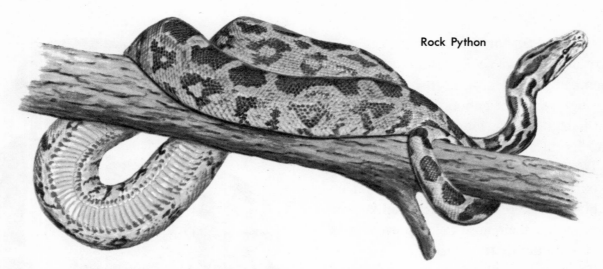

Rock Python

Pythons and Boas—Snake Giants

These are the giants among snakes. They are also the most primitive. Some of the pythons have traces of hind legs just in front of the tail, and their skeletons have "hips," which are lacking in all other kinds of snakes.

Boas and pythons are similar but inhabit different parts of the world—the boas living in the South American tropics and subtropics, the pythons in similar regions in Africa and Asia. Among their differences: Boas do not have teeth at the front of the lower jaw; pythons do. Boas have only one row of scales on the underside of the body; pythons have two. Pythons lay eggs; boas give birth to their young—that is, they keep the eggs inside the body until they hatch.

Both boas and pythons kill their prey by constriction. They wrap coils of their body around their victim and then squeeze tightly, causing death by suffocation and by stopping the circulation of blood. When the prey is dead, or nearly so, the snake swallows it whole, starting at the head. Both snakes become sluggish after eating and do not become active again until the meal is completely digested. This may require several weeks if the snake has stuffed its stomach with a deer, a pig, or some other large animal.

A female python is the only snake that incubates her eggs. She pushes the eggs into a pile, then coils her body around them, using her head to cover them. Snakes are cold-blooded, their body temperature the same as, or very close to, the air temperature of their surroundings. But while she is incubating her eggs, a female python's body temperature will rise to as much as ten degrees higher than the surrounding air temperature. It may be nearly three months before the eggs hatch. All this while, the female stays with them, leaving only to get water.

Anacondas are South American boas. They are reported to reach a length of forty feet, but in this case, both the stories and the snake are believed to have been stretched. Anacondas do grow to a length of more than thirty feet, however, and they are the heaviest of all snakes, attaining a weight of more than four hundred pounds. This giant is almost always found in or near water, and it does not hesitate to attack animals as large as jaguars.

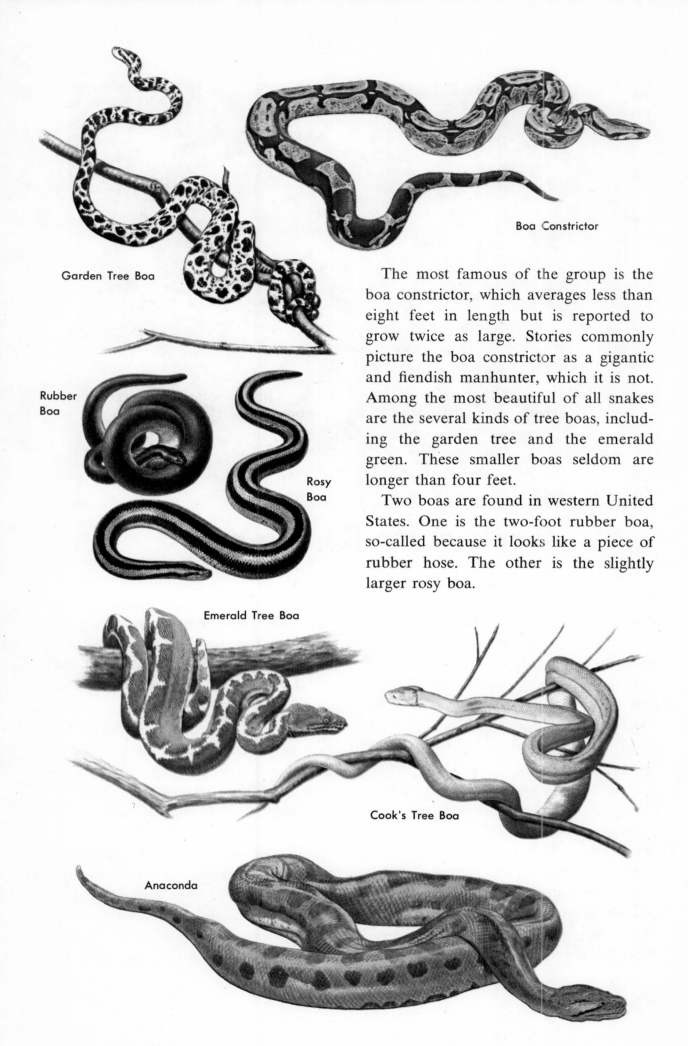

Boa Constrictor

Garden Tree Boa

Rubber
Boa

Rosy
Boa

The most famous of the group is the boa constrictor, which averages less than eight feet in length but is reported to grow twice as large. Stories commonly picture the boa constrictor as a gigantic and fiendish manhunter, which it is not. Among the most beautiful of all snakes are the several kinds of tree boas, including the garden tree and the emerald green. These smaller boas seldom are longer than four feet.

Two boas are found in western United States. One is the two-foot rubber boa, so-called because it looks like a piece of rubber hose. The other is the slightly larger rosy boa.

Emerald Tree Boa

Cook's Tree Boa

Anaconda

Alligator

Giants of the Reptile World

Alligators and crocodiles are the most fearsome of all the reptiles because of their tremendous size, and, of course, they can be extremely dangerous if approached too closely.

There are two kinds of alligators. One lives in southeastern United States, the other in China. The alligator has a broad snout, and none of its lower teeth extend up and over the upper jaw.

Several dozen kinds of crocodiles live in saltwater regions of the subtropics and tropics around the world. A crocodile has a long, slim snout, and the fourth tooth of its lower jaw comes outside the upper jaw when the mouth is closed. Gavials, of southeastern Asia, are closely related to crocodiles. Mainly fish eaters, they have very thin, long snouts.

South American caimans are close relatives of alligators. Young caimans are sometimes sold to the public as baby alligators, which are now protected by law in the United States.

Today, an American alligator longer than twelve feet is exceptionally rare, though there are records from the past of nineteen-footers. Several of the crocodiles exceed a length of twenty feet, as do the gavials.

Alligators and crocodiles appear to be slow, sluggish animals, but for short distances, they can move with astonishing speed. They make fast dashes if angered enough to attack, when they are frightened and running away, or when they are after prey. In the water, they fold their legs close to their body and swim by moving their whole body back and forth. Most of the power for swimming comes from their tail, which is also their most dangerous weapon.

These great lizardlike animals are remarkably fitted for their life in water. The air-breathing channel from their nostrils is completely separated from their mouth, which permits them to chew underwater without taking water into their lungs. Both the nostrils and the eyes are located on bulges above the main surface of the head. This permits the animals to see and breathe while keeping their head and body underwater.

Crocodiles and alligators lay eggs. The female alligator makes an elaborate nest—a mound of decaying vegetation, in the center of which she lays several dozen rubbery white eggs. On top of the eggs, she piles more debris, until the mound is as much as three or four feet across and equally high. The heat of the decaying vegetation incubates the eggs.

The female stays nearby and chases off intruders. When she hears a squeaking inside the mound, a signal that baby alligators are making their way out of the shells, she pulls away the vegetation to help them escape.

Gavial

Caiman

Nile Crocodile

Fact and Fiction

Snakes are *not* slimy.
Their bodies are covered with dry scales.

Toads do *not* cause warts.
A toad's skin does give off a secretion, and this can be irritating—even poisonous in some kinds of toads.

Snakes *will* crawl over a horsehair rope— or any other kind of rope.
Placing a rope around a campsite will *not* keep snakes out.

Snakes do *not* hypnotize their prey.
They do seem to stare, simply because they have no eyelids.

***All* poisonous snakes do *not* have triangular-shaped heads.**
Some harmless snakes do have triangular heads, but coral snakes, cobras, and others which are very poisonous do not have triangular heads.

A snake *can* bite underwater.
This is especially true of snakes that feed in the water.

A snake does *not* bite or sting with its tongue.
The tongue is soft and harmless, and the snake uses it to help it to smell.

A snake or turtle with its head cut off does *not* live until sundown.
Because of its simple nervous system, however, it will twitch for a while, though dead.

It *never* really rains toads and frogs.
In heavy rains, these animals may be flooded from their hiding places and suddenly appear in great numbers.

Rattlesnakes do *not* add just *one* button a year to their rattle.
They add a new button each time they shed their skin, which may be as often as three or four times a year.

Glass snakes are really legless lizards.
Contrary to legend, they can *not* break themselves into many pieces and then put themselves together again.